CRIME AND PUNISHMENT
AT BEAUMARIS

CRIME AND PUNISHMENT AT BEAUMARIS

By

Margaret Hughes

ISBN: 1-84527-091-6

Cover design: Sian Parri

Published by
Gwasg Carreg Gwalch, 12 Iard yr Orsaf, Llanrwst,
Wales LL26 0EH.
℡ 01492 642031   📠 01492 641502
🖰 books@carreg-gwalch.co.uk   Web site: www.carreg-gwalch.co.uk

Crime and Punishment at Beaumaris

Early Days

Beaumaris Court House bears the date 1614 and the Gaol 1829. But the story of the enforcement of law and order in Anglesey begins with the reign of the Welsh Princes, centuries earlier.

In those days Anglesey was divided into commotes, a commote being part of a larger area known as a Hundred. Each commote had its own court. The business transacted there was varied, from the collection of revenues and fines to the maintenance of order. Two officials were in charge – the bailiff (Welsh *rhaglaw*) and the beadle (*rhingyll*). It was the bailiff's responsibility to supervise rent collections and to arrest felons. As time progressed, the beadle assumed more importance and took over some of these tasks.

As well as the commote courts there were several others operating privately as the need arose. The church court heard ecclesiastical cases. A manorial court existed, as did the Tourn and the Hundred court. Administration of law and order was arbitrary in those far-off days until, in 1284, the Statute of Wales created a new overall pattern by introducing a system of administrative units which were similar throughout Wales.

Gwynedd was divided into three counties – Anglesey, being one. The purpose of the counties was to serve as the financial channel to the Crown and to administer law and order. The commote was still the basic unit and this

English-style organisation was built upon it. New officers were created to operate the new system in each county. Anglesey had its first Lord Lieutenant, a Sheriff, High Constables and Petty Constables.

The Lord Lieutenant was the head of the county, commanding all the armed force of his area for the King. Next in precedence came the Sheriff, appointed by the Crown for one year, and under him the High Constables who were appointed by the Quarter Sessions. Petty Constables collected the county rate which was then passed to their superiors and eventually to the Sheriff who made his return to the Crown. The Sheriff's tasks included sitting at the courts and he was the Keeper of the county gaol situated at Beaumaris Castle. The High Constables were legally obliged to bring to justice all those within their own areas who offended against the law.

Under this system a county court was created, and Anglesey experienced its first Great Sessions (Assizes) and Quarter Sessions.

By the end of the 13th century a legal framework existed which would be adapted to suit the needs of later years.

For the purpose of this review of crime and punishment at Beaumaris, the work of the Assizes and Quarter Sessions will be the main areas of discussion.

Beaumaris was the largest township on the island. It was a port and a commercial centre. It was reasonably well defended with a castle which, although incomplete, was of a state-of-the-art design unknown elsewhere in Britain. The town also came to be regarded as Anglesey's administrative centre.

Quarter Sessions were ordered by statute to be held during the first weeks after St Michael, the Epiphany, the Clause of Easter and the Translation of St Thomas the Martyr. These four meetings were observed strictly in

Beaumaris. They met, along with the two Assize courts each year, in the castle where the Sheriff lived and where there was a dungeon.

As time passed, the condition of the castle fabric deteriorated. The Court House was built in 1614, also a purpose-built gaol on the edge of The Green. Although both new buildings may have improved conditions in Beaumaris to a degree, prisons throughout Britain were places of filth, degradation and humiliation still operated within a tradition set down years before the Statute of Wales came into force. It was time for reform. The man who instigated this reform was John Howard of Bedford.

John Howard was born in 1726. He spent his early life in Cardington near Bedford where his father owned a small estate. His parents both died when John and his brother were young, leaving them the estate and a sizeable fortune. John toured the continent. He married when he was twenty years old, but his wife died shortly afterwards.

John Howard's philanthropy began when he built model brick cottages for his estate workers and arranged for the education of their children.

Although he was a sick man for most of his life, he travelled widely. In 1773 he was appointed Sheriff of Bedfordshire. Then began his life-long interest in prison reform. As he researched the living conditions appertaining to prisons he was shocked to find that those held in gaol pending trial and found not guilty at that trial, were still kept in gaol until they had paid the gaoler his fee for their release. This practice was widespread, and as some prisoners held were so poor that they could not find the release fee, their stay in prison was lengthened considerably until they were able to pay.

John Howard's work, as he visited every gaol in Britain, attracted widespread attention and he was called to give evidence of his findings before a House of

Commons committee in 1774. The government later congratulated him on his 'humanity and zeal'. Bills followed, concerning the abolition of gaolers' fees and the better health of prisoners.

When Howard visited Beaumaris gaol his recommendations of 1770 ordered 'that a strong wall be built between the House of Correction and Mr Jones's garden to an equal height with the other wall for the better preservation of the gaol and said House of Correction and for the safe custody of the prisoners therein'.

The Act 'for Preserving the Health of Prisoners and preventing the Gaol Distemper' required gaols and prisons to be kept clean and in proper repair. Referring to Beaumaris gaol on The Green it was ordered 'that the state of repair of this County Gaol and the cells and wards and Rooms therein be examined into and sufficiently repaired and the walls and ceiling thereof scraped and whitewashed once a year regularly, washed and kept clean'.

Bailiffs' accounts for 1786 list the cost of materials for repairing the fabric of the building to bring it up to the required standard . . .

'The materials – stone, gravel, lime – cost £6. 2. 4d.'

In addition to £1.8.6d for 1,000 bricks to make the chimney, £3.13.11½d was spent on the prison in 1787 and similar amounts in subsequent years.

Gaols were divided into a prison for criminals, and a House of Correction, the latter being the place where debtors, vagrants and prisoners who had committed less serious moral offences against society were kept. However, in Beaumaris, their treatment differed little from that meted out to criminals in the other section.

A new chapter in the story of law and order in

Anglesey opened in 1829 when the gaunt prison building in Steeple Lane, designed by John Hansom (of Hansom cab fame) and Welch, two York architects, opened to receive convicts. These two architects were also the designers of the Bulkeley Arms Hotel and the handsome Victoria Terrace of houses alongside, built on the site of the demolished first prison. But more of that later.

Cause and Effect

What accounted for the crimes perpetrated in Anglesey which resulted in trial and prison sentences during the 17th, 18th and 19th centuries? Human nature, no doubt, which does not alter with circumstances or the years. But social conditions, certainly, as times of extreme poverty brought to the surface much of what today would be regarded as petty crime – stealing small items, clothes, food, farm and household goods, by those who had no money to buy them. The price of food rocketed following the Napoleonic Wars and work was difficult to find, making it a desperately hard time for many who were already poor. As the wars ended there was less demand for goods to supply the army and navy, and as men returned to the land, work could not be found for them all.

The economic state of Anglesey during the early years of the nineteenth century gave cause for much petty crime. The war against the French had resulted in a shortage of foodstuffs and agricultural produce, so prices rose and the plight of the poor was increased. Rents were also increased. There was great hardship after the poor harvest of 1816, and certain Anglesey landowners did reduce some rents to their tenants, recognising that hardship, but not all. A ship carrying corn was boarded at Amlwch by a party of desperately hungry men who removed the tiller to make sure the ship was unable to sail. Soldiers were called in to deal with the trouble and six of the ringleaders were arrested and held in Beaumaris Gaol. One of the troublemakers escaped from the old Gaol on The Green, three were found guilty and received short sentences and the other two were released.

Poverty fed crime. There were instances of petty theft – poaching, stealing a loaf of bread, eggs from a farm, an article of clothing. The number of children dependent on the parish for support increased, and many of those children were prompted to steal. The last months of 1852 saw the wettest Anglesey had experienced within living memory. Crops were ruined, fields flooded, cottages damaged.

Although the great expansion of the copper industry at Amlwch had resulted in more jobs, of a kind, living conditions for the workers there were abysmal as their wages were low and their homes were often no more than shacks thrown together in Amlwch village which had developed from a handful of houses to a sprawling town in a matter of a few years. An influx of 'foreigners' looking for work there and at the port in Holyhead added to the crime problem.

Those most affected by crime were land – and property – owners. Until the 1850s Anglesey had no police force. Apprehending wrongdoers was a hit and miss affair. Many offenders were never brought to justice. But there were rumblings of discontent among Anglesey property-owners, some of whom set up their own associations to deal with the problem – what might today be regarded as a kind of 'neighbourhood watch'. The associations warned would-be miscreants of the fate awaiting them if they were caught, and offered rewards to those who apprehended culprits.

These associations were particularly active after the end of the Napoleonic Wars. Property-owners who banded together paid a subscription to the association,

out of which rewards were paid. In a newspaper of 1817 the following notice appeared under the heading 'Beaumaris Association for the Apprehension of Felons'
. . .

'Whereas several Felonies, Larcenies and Depredations of various kinds have been committed in and about the neighbourhood of Beaumaris, and the offenders have almost always escaped justice, for want of immediate and effective prosecution thereof, the several persons whose names are hereunto subscribed, associating themselves together in order to prevent and suppress every kind of Felony and Larceny (as far as in them lie) have agreed to raise and maintain a Fund for the prosecution of such offenders, committed against the property of them, or either of them. And for managing the affairs of this association the following Gentlemen, or any three of them, are appointed a committee, viz., The Mayor and Bailiffs for the time being, Sir Robert Williams, Baronet, John Bodychan Sparrow, John Williams and Rowland Williams. And the said committee do hereby offer information in the Premises, as shall lead to the recovery of the property stolen and the apprehension of the offenders in the undermentioned cases, to be paid on the conviction of such offenders, by JOHN JONES of Rating Row, Attorney at Law, Treasurer in the following manner:

Highway Robbery, or the feloniously breaking or
    entering any house in the night time 5.5.0
The like in the day time 3.3.0
The feloniously stealing, killing maiming or
    wounding any horse, mare or gelding 5.5.0
The like of any bull, ox, cow, steer, heifer, calf,
    sheep, lamb or hog 1.1.0
Any grand or petty larceny 1.1.0

The stealing of any poultry 1.1.0
Stealing any gate, pale, or rail or any iron work
    or other thing belonging thereto, or breaking
    any hedge or other fence 1.1.0
Robbing any orchard or garden or stealing or
    maliciously destroying any turnips, potatoes,
    parsnips, carrots, cabbages or peas, growing
    in any enclosed ground 1.1.0
All persons having any Demand on the above Society
are desired to send their accounts to the Treasurer, at
least ten days before the first of March and to attend
the committee at 10 o'clock in the morning of that day,
at the Bulls Head Inn in Beaumaris, when the same
shall be examined of any of the subscribers as may
attend.'

Then followed a list of subscribers to the Association,
each having paid ten shillings to be a member.

A similar association was set up in Amlwch after the
1817 riot in the town. In 1822 this Association gave due
notice to any would-be felon in no uncertain terms,
through fly-posting locally. Anyone accused would be
tried at Beaumaris.

'AMLWCH ASSOCIATION FOR THE PROSECUTION
OF FELONS
1st March 1822
'Whereas by an Act of Parliament passed in the first
Year of the Reign of King George the Fourth, for the
summary punishment, in certain cases, of Persons
wilfully or maliciously damaging or committing
Trespass on public or private Property – it is enacted
that if any Person or Persons shall wilfully or
maliciously do or commit any Damage, Injury, or
Spoil, to or upon any Building, Fence, Hedge, Gate,
Stile, Tree, Wood, Underwood, Orchard, Garden,

Nursery Ground, Crops, Vegetables, Plants, Land, or other Matter or Thing growing or being thereon, or to or upon real or personal property of any kind soever, and shall be thereof convicted in the manner in the said Act set forth, shall forfeit and pay to the Person or Persons aggrieved, such a Sum of Money, not exceeding £5, as therein directed; and in default of Payment of the same, and Expenses, the Justice convicting the Party shall and may commit the Offender or Offenders to the common Gaol, there to be kept to hard Labour for three Months.'

'Therefore NOTICE IS HEREBY GIVEN That the Members of the above Association are determined to avail themselves of the Benefit of the above Act, by prosecuting and punishing all such Offenders as they shall find guilty of committing any of the Trespasses therein set forth.

ROBERT PRICHARD, Treasurer and Secretary to the said Association.'

These two Associations, and others like them, did deter crime, but it was to be some forty years before an efficient police force began to make significant inroads into the crime statistics on the island.

Inadequate policing in early days and the fact that laws varied from area to area and so gave a criminal the chance to escape charge if he moved from the scene of the crime before being apprehended, gave birth to the 'hue and cry'. A band of men from the parish where the felony was perpetrated would give chase, sometimes over many miles, doing their detective work as they went, and gaining help from other parishes and townships on the way. This happened in Anglesey when Richard Bulkeley was making for Penmaenmawr when he met Major Richard Cheadle on the Lavan Sands. They had an argument and swords were drawn. Bulkeley was murdered. Cheadle rode away without stopping until he reached Nantwich in Cheshire. Meanwhile the Beaumaris Hue and Cry chased him as far as Chester where the Chester Hue and Cry took up the chase and Cheadle was eventually found in Nantwich, apprehended, and taken to Chester castle.

Beaumaris Court House – Quarter Sessions

After Beaumaris Court House opened in 1614 the Quarter Sessions and Great Sessions (Assizes) were held there.

Today one can only imagine the building as it was when first built, as additions have been made over the years. The outer surface of the stone work has been subjected to plastering and colouring.

When the Sheriff lived in the castle, court sessions were held there. But deterioration of the fabric and its unsuitability caused the Court House to be built. The original was a large rectangular building with a vestibule at the entrance. The present walls, roof trusses and the heavy studded door at the entrance are the originals. In time, the east end was extended to create the Grand Jury Room, a more elegant addition, and a projecting wing on the south side near the Judge's seat. Later a Judge's Room and Petty Jury Room and gallery on the north side were also added, along with the tiny prisoner's room opposite, where the unfortunate accused waited to be taken into court for the hearing. The main hall was divided into two by the seven-foot high iron railing which separates the business end of the court room from the stone-flagged public area. Against the south wall an enclosed seat, reached by steps, was built in the 18th century to accommodate the Mayor and bailiffs who then had a clear view of proceedings as they looked down from above the railing. During the 19th century, a small records room was opened above the vestibule, reached by a flight of wooden steps from the south west corner of the public area.

Quarter Sessions, as the name implies, were held four times a year before a Justice and Recorder. These tried misdemeanours and petty crimes, now called summary cases. They also heard disputes over property and sanctioned official payments when necessary. Felonies, now referred to as indictable offences, were heard before a Judge at Assizes, held twice a year.

Justices of the Peace presiding over the Quarter Sessions were chosen from the Welsh gentry. Their jurisdiction was over minor crimes, but occasionally they were responsible for quelling a riot. Many were bilingual and members of powerful families. The Bulkeley family of Beaumaris was one of these. They could often influence the choice of Justices from the lesser gentry who considered the post to be of social advantage as well as a means of underlining their control of law and order among the yeomen and tenants. So most took their responsibilities seriously.

Quarter Session records give a vivid picture of the work of the court over a long period of time. For example, between 1768 and 1788 there were cases of larceny, burglary, bastardy, desertion from the militia and escape from prison.

Articles stolen were often of negligible value, yet punishment could be cruel in the extreme. This was becoming a public scandal and was one reason for the reforms which slowly came into being. In fact, the intrinsic value of articles stolen seems to have been purposely undervalued by the juries occasionally, so as to bring the total value below twelve pence and so save the culprit the severest punishment, which could be the death penalty. A flogging was preferred and often used. 'A sound whipping' involved the culprit being stripped from the waist upwards and set upon with the birch. A flogging, for a more serious crime, was inflicted publicly, either in the market place of the town or village where the crime took place, or it could be administered 'ambulando' through the streets. The gaolers or the bailiffs administered the punishment.

In 1785 a man stole an iron chain valued at five pence. As well as being committed to gaol for three months he was publicly whipped once each month, the first time in Beaumaris, the second 'in the village of Amlwch in the usual manner from High Gate'. The journey between the places would have been done on horseback.

At the 1788 Sessions a prisoner received three floggings for stealing part of a plough to the value of sixpence. A woman was publicly whipped for stealing 'two linen caps, one flannel petticoat and one yard of black riband of the value of 4d'.

Quarter Sessions could sentence a guilty person to a period in prison 'with hard labour'. Hard labour could be work done within the gaol over long hours each day, on a poor diet, with little respite. Sometimes men were sent to do their stint on the River Thames 'to raise sand, soil and gravel from and cleansing the River Thames and other services for the benefit of the navigation of the said river'. This type of hard labour had been sanctioned by an Act of Parliament in 1776 and there is evidence in the records of men having been sent from Beaumaris.

If the accused was dealt with summarily by the Justice rather than for his case to go to the Assizes, he might avoid the death penalty. Instead he might expect the Justice to sentence him to transportation.

Women, as well as men, received this punishment. This happened to two women convicted of petty larceny. They were ordered to be 'transported to one of His Majesty's plantations in America, there to remain for the space of seven years'.

This was no soft option. The voyage could be hell, cooped up as they were in the hold of an unsanitary ship and at the beck and call of a brutal crew who used them as prostitutes. After seven years of hard labour on the plantation, being treated like slaves, there was little likelihood of either of these women having saved enough money to pay their passage home.

One type of case heard in the Beaumaris Court House was especially associated with Anglesey. 'Cornish lamping' was carried out on the west coast, where a gang of thieves known as 'Lladron Crigyll' *(Crigyll Robbers)* operated. This was an area of frequent shipwrecks at a time when sea charting was poor if not non-existent, and the coastline treacherous in bad weather for vulnerable sailing ships. Lamps were fastened to the necks of cattle grazing along the shoreline; the constantly moving lights tempted a ship not familiar with the coast and in difficulties in a storm to come closer to the shore where submerged rocks could cause shipwreck. This happened in 1740 when four ringleaders of the gang were captured.

Wrecks and their cargoes were, officially, government property. But to a desperately poor population around Rhosneigr they were riches not to be ignored, and some believed it within their rights to salvage what they could. The ringleaders were accused of plundering the ship *Loveday and Betty*. But all was pandemonium in Beaumaris Court House as the trial opened. The Assize Judge was drunk throughout the trial. The men had commissioned a brilliant lawyer to defend them, and other members of the gang went along to support their ringleaders, where they terrified the jury. The result was an acquittal, received with much jubilation.

In 1778 a ship, *Charming Jenny*, went ashore in a storm on the same coast with the captain's wife drowning in a rock pool as she attempted to reach the shore, while the Crigyll Robbers carried goods off the ship. The captain must have been aware of the trial which had taken place in Beaumaris nearly forty years earlier, and decided to take his case to an English court at Shrewsbury where he believed he was more likely to receive justice.

There was one loophole for a man accused of a serious crime to avoid imprisonment or worse. He could be pardoned if he promised to enter the King's service.

Offenders were often too poor to pay imposed fines, so severe pain was inflicted as punishment. Burning the hand was widely done and in varying degrees depending upon the seriousness of the crime.

There is no doubt that punishment did not fit the crime and the public was becoming more aware of this. Sometimes, juries at Quarter Sessions refused to convict a defendant, even when it was obvious that he was guilty, because they felt the punishment to be unrealistic.

Not everyone tried at Beaumaris Court House completed a sentence. Some were pardoned. For this, the Keeper had to provide evidence of good behaviour before a petition would be made to the Monarch by the visiting Justices on behalf of the prisoner.

In the case of Robert Jones the following official pardon was received . . .

'Whereas Robert Jones was at the Quarter Sessions holden for the County of Anglesea (sic) in July 1845 convicted of Receiving Stolen Goods and sentenced to be imprisoned for Two Years for the same We in consideration of some circumstances humbly represented unto Us are Graciously pleased to extend Grace and Mercy unto him and to Grant him Our Free Pardons for the crime of which he stands convicted. Our Will and Pleasure therefore that you cause him the said Robert Jones to be forthwith discharged out of Custody and for so doing this shall be your warrant. April 1847 in the Tenth year of our Reign Her

Majesty's Command To Our Trusty and well beloved Keeper of the House of Correction for the County of Anglesea and others whom it may concern.'

So Robert Jones served nine months of his two years' sentence before receiving his pardon.

In the case of Griffith Roberts, we know more about the circumstances of his pardon. Included in the file is a statement from the Keeper of the Gaol as to his 'quiet and industrious behaviour'. He was convicted for larceny in 1842. His plea for pardon reads . . .

'Your humble petitioner hopes through your tender mercies towards my wife and young family who are entirely destitute of maintenance and support on account of my confinement I hope and trust that your Worships will mitigate and shorten my sentence according to your wise discretion.'

The Keeper's statement commented that Griffith Roberts had, during his incarceration, spent time reviewing his folly and was determined to start a new life on his release.

'Gaoler wanted'

In preparation for the opening of the new gaol an advertisement was placed in several newspapers, inviting applications for the post of Keeper, or Gaoler. This appeared in the *North Wales Chronicle, Chester Chronicle, Chester Journal, Shrewsbury Journal, Liverpool Courier* and *Cambrian* . . .

'GAOLER WANTED
A person conversant in the Welsh language will be preferred. The gaoler's wife discharging the duties of Matron. Persons wishing for further information are to apply to Mr Jones, Town Clerk, Beaumaris. Persons applying producing satisfactory certification of their characters.'

There were over twenty applicants, from Wales and England, some with experience, others wishing to move from their present employment where they could see no future. The Justices met and weighed each application on its merits. They chose Hugh Jones, a mariner from Beaumaris, and his wife, Elizabeth, as Matron. They were to live in the prison and would be paid £52 per annum in quarterly instalments. The court order giving official sanction to the appointment also carried a long list of rules which the couple had to acknowledge, including . . .

'He (the gaoler) shall not nor shall any person in trust

for him nor employed by him sell or have any benefit or advantage from the sale of any article to any Prisoner nor shall he directly or indirectly have any interest in any contract or agreement for the supply of the Prison.'

New Prison – New Rules

Before 1823, the date of the Gaol Act, prisons were the insanitary places visited by John Howard, carelessly run, where regulations were slack if not non-existent. Howard remarked on visiting the prison on The Green in Beaumaris that no water or straw was provided for the inmates in the duty rooms, and while it was marginally better than others in the country, much improvement was needed. The gaoler, he said, took a fee of five shillings from each prisoner who could afford it, and held a licence to sell beer to them. Those who could not afford to pay went without. The Gaol Act quashed this long-standing practice.

As a result of prison reform in Britain following Howard's visits, the new Beaumaris Gaol had to be operated according to a set of rules. Compared with the lackadaisical organisation previously, when any relaxation of harsh treatment depended largely on the mood of the gaoler, life in Steeple Lane promised to be different.

An order dated 'THURSDAY the Third Day of SEPTEMBER One Thousand Eight Hundred and Twenty Nine' stipulated how the new gaol was to be run, with a resident Keeper as superintendent. He was ordered to visit every cell at least once a day, and if he wished to visit a female prisoner he had to be accompanied by the Matron or another female in the Matron's absence.

The Keeper had to write a daily Journal in which he recorded any punishments authorised.

The sexes were separated so as to prevent them from 'seeing, conversing or holding any intercourse with each other'. Still further segregation occurred as the various classes of prisoners were grouped together, 'care being taken that prisoners of the several classes do not intermix with each other'.

Every prisoner sentenced to hard labour was to be employed 'from six o'clock in the morning, or as soon after as there is sufficient light, to six in the evening if light be so long; out of this time the prisoner shall in all cases be allowed one hour for 'dinner, and when the length of the day is such as to admit of their beginning to work earlier than seven, they shall be allowed another hour for breakfast. They are not to be employed on Christmas Day or Good Friday'.

Prisoners under charge or conviction of any crime, and prisoners receiving any allowance for employment from the county, had to attend Divine Service in the chapel on Sunday, 'Debtors not attending shall be locked up for security during the time of Service.'

No prisoner was to be put in irons, except in cases of urgent necessity, and then their use should not be for more than four days.

In abiding by these rules, the Keeper was to maintain constant contact with the visiting Justices, so the autonomous rule of the gaoler came to an end.

The maintenance of prisoners was effected in different ways, depending on their ability to work. Those who worked and were paid a small wage for doing so had to use that money to keep themselves in food and clothing. Those who were unable to find sufficient paid work (stone-cutting or oakum picking for the men, spinning or weaving or mat making for the women) within the prison had to rely on the Justices at Quarter Sessions making them an allowance. If under the care of the prison doctor, he or she was allowed a special diet. Debtors received no such county allowance, nor did those awaiting trial, but they had to maintain themselves, depending on family and friends. The Rules stipulated 'They shall be allowed to procure for themselves and to receive at proper hours any goods, bedding, clothing, or any other necessaries subject to a strict examination.'

Prisoners were allowed visitors, but visits were strictly recorded and regulated.

Visitors to the prison could expect to be searched by the Keeper or the Matron should there be any doubt of the visitor's innocence. Packets brought in to the gaol were opened to verify their contents.

New inmates were examined by the prison surgeon before being allocated a cell. No prisoner was discharged at the end of his sentence if he was suffering from any disease. The clothing of every prisoner was fumigated before being stored away, pending his release, and he (or she) would be made to don prison uniform.

Cleanliness was considered important. 'The walls and ceilings of the wards, cells, rooms and passages used by the prisoners should be scraped and lime-washed at least once in the year; the day rooms, work rooms, passages and sleeping cells shall be washed or cleaned once a week or oftener if requisite. Convenient places for the prisoners to wash themselves shall be provided with an adequate allowance of soap, towels, and combs. All prisoners shall be allowed as much air and exercise as may be deemed proper for the preservation of their health.'

Alcohol was not permitted unless the prison surgeon prescribed it.

Prisoners were forbidden to offer bribes for favours, a practice rife up to the end of the 18th century when gaolers held sway in the prison hierarchy.

Under the Rules the Keeper had power to punish those

rebelling against any prison rule. This punishment was usually close confinement in a solitary cell, the prisoner existing on bread and water for up to a maximum of three days. These cases had to be noted in the Keeper's journal and reported to the visiting Justices.

'The surgeon shall enquire into the mental as well as bodily state of every Prisoner, and when he shall have reason to believe that the mind or body is materially affected by the discipline, treatment, or diet, particularly of such as are in solitary confinement, he shall inform the Keeper thereof, and enter his observations and directions in his Journal, which shall be an authority to the Keeper for altering the discipline, treatment or diet of any prisoner until the next visit of a visiting Justice, who shall enquire into the case and make orders accordingly.'

Work for the prisoner was considered important. The Keeper had to obtain materials for the inmates, and keep an inventory of these for the Justices.

Debtors had different treatment in their daily lives to that given to the criminals. The Rules stated 'Debtors shall not be made subject to any further degree of rigour or restraint than such as shall be found necessary for the good government, proper condition, and cleanly state of the Prison'.

The work of keeping the prison clean was done by the inmates, who carried out their tasks throughout the building; debtors, however, had to keep within their own ward and not mix with others. No water or fuel was to be wasted.

Sleeping rooms were opened at 6 a.m. in the summer and an hour before sunrise in the winter. All the prisoners were locked in their sleeping rooms at nine o'clock at night. A bell rang to announce the Keeper's approach to lock up – locks were on the outside of all the doors.

Various prison reforms throughout the 19th century brought a measure of ease to the harsh conditions of

Beaumaris Gaol, but new rules could never disperse the fear that the gaunt stone walls aroused in the Anglesey community.

Life in the New Prison

The inmates of Beaumaris Gaol were, in the main, petty criminals who had been incarcerated on the orders of the Quarter Sessions, and those awaiting trial. Occasionally there were the more serious cases, convicted at the Assizes. Debtors were also held there until their debts had been paid.

Those who came fresh from trial were escorted in chains from the Court House along the streets, probably gazed at curiously and perhaps vocally derided by anyone who happened to be near at the time. This would be the last they would see of the world outside the high prison wall in Steeple Lane until the end of their sentence.

A Report on Prisons carried out by government inspectors was published in 1852, and had this to record concerning Beaumaris Gaol . . .

'On the left hand side of the entrance hall, which is unnecessarily spacious, is a large room used for the meetings of the magistrates, the apartment of the Keeper being on the left. The hall is shut off from the prison by a barred iron partition through which as the outer door is constantly open, air is very freely admitted into the interior of the building.'

'The prison consists of three wings; that to the west contains on the ground floor a reception ward for men, a similar cell for women . . . a day room and airing yard for male debtors, the hospital and store for oakum.'

'The south wing contains on the ground floor a refractory cell with a tiled floor in which prisoners are kept only by day – it is not dark, and in point of situation is one of the best in the prison; also a day room and airing yard for prisoners before trial in which the only untried prisoner was confined; and the day room of convicted prisoners not sentenced to labour, of whom there were three at the time of my visit.'

'On the ground floor of this division is the chapel, partitioned in a radiated form for prisoners of the several classes.'

'The south wing on the upper floor is devoted to a bathroom, a room for the turnkey, and eight cells for untried prisoners and misdemeanants. The cells are paved with tiles and have hammocks and bedding, including sheets. The ground floor of the east wing comprises the cookhouse, two rooms for females, the first being a day room and the second being unappropriated. The other side of the same passage contains a day room for convicted prisoners sentenced to hard labour . . . in this room five men were engaged in picking oakum. This wing, on the upper floor, contains four cells for women and the remaining five for men.'

A prisoner's first impression on entering the forbidding building was one of gloom and despondency. There is little information available now to know how this would have compared with the atmosphere at the previous gaol on The Green, but we can assume that prison rules laid down for the new gaol did ensure a measure of order in its administration.

On arrival, the prisoner was taken into the small reception room behind the iron grill separating him from his freedom. Here he was stripped and given a bath – an experience which was unfamiliar to many! He was given prison clothes, his own taken away to be fumigated and stored until his release. Those awaiting trial, miscreants and debtors, wore their own clothing. Any personal possessions were also stored. Reading one of the Personal Property Lists gives one an insight into how little some prisoners possessed apart from the clothes they wore – coat, vest, drawers, flannel shirt, boots, shoes or clogs, stockings, handkerchief, braces, top coat, tobacco, pipes, pencil, comb, knife, key, purse, and, in the case of prisoner John Lower, two pawn tickets. There is no mention of money.

The prisoner was then weighed and given a medical examination by the prison surgeon. All this was done in SILENCE, as notices on the walls ordered, before he was taken to his 'sleeping room' or cell.

In 1852 the inspector wrote . . .

'The whole accommodation amounts to twenty cells for male and four for female prisoners. None of the cells are warmed, but there are small fireplaces in the day rooms. The cells are generally of sufficient size to admit of their being certified for separate confinement if they were only provided with the means of artificial heat, which is scarcely less necessary in their present application as the stone walls in the humid climate of Wales must be very damp and cold, especially in the winter season.'

'The prison appears to be well drained, and its records would not appear to support the opinion of its unhealthiness which has been sometimes expressed, although its site in point of elevation does not seem to have been well selected. From the defective supervision arising from the small number of officers, attempts at escape are likely to be made, but the wall being surmounted by large loose pieces of slate placed vertically in its whole circuit, it would probably be found impossible to scale it.'

In fact, the inspector was proved wrong, as one such attempt was made in 1859 when Owen Morris jumped from the top of the wall to the street below. He broke a leg in the fall. But he struggled to reach a nearby wood where he hid until he was found the next day, and taken back to the prison. He had succeeded in making a rope from oakum obtained in the workroom, a little at a time. As he was due to be released he was wearing his own clothes and, but for his accident, might have been able to get away.

Staff at the prison mentioned in the 1852 Report were the governor, chaplain, surgeon, matron, one turnkey who was also the schoolmaster, chaplain's clerk, and clerk to the visiting Justices.

The inspector ended with this comment . . .

'The prison presents capabilities of improvement. By the conversion of day rooms into cells and the proper warming of the prison, a sufficient number of cells capable of being certified might be procured in which the ordinary number of prisoners might be placed in separate confinement. Whether this be done or not, the appointment of another turnkey and schoolmaster appears to be absolutely necessary to maintain proper discipline, and to effect any effectual instruction to the prisoners.'

Prison diet was frugal. Debtors and those awaiting trial had to provide for themselves, depending on the willingness of family and friends. Convicts had a small subsistence allowance from the county which was paid until 1865, after which all diet expenses in the prison were reviewed. If a prisoner's sentence was only a few days long, he could expect the breakfast oatmeal gruel, bread and water. Longer-term prisoners had to have their health considered so were given a more varied diet. Their breakfast consisted of gruel and bread, which was also the menu for their supper. Dinner was bread and soup on three days; meat, potatoes and bread for four days with extra if they were on hard labour.

Although even this small amount was an improvement on the food available at the prison on The Green, it was hardly enough for a hungry man or woman, and the 1852 Report commented on complaints received by the inspector . . .

> 'The prisoners very generally complained that they have not their stipulated allowance of meat in the soup. On enquiry I found the complaint to be well founded, as the meat of which the soup is made on one day is given to the prisoners as solid meat on the next. The diet is besides objectionable, on the ground of the same amount of food being given to all prisoners for terms exceeding fourteen days, whatever may be the length of their confinement, whereby an unnecessary quantity of food is given to the short-sentenced prisoner. The dietary has not received the sanction of the Secretary of State, as required by law.'

In 1869 male prisoners sentenced to hard labour for periods of more than three months were given a pint of oatmeal gruel and six ounces of bread for breakfast; four ounces of cooked meat without bone, a pound of potatoes and six ounces of bread for dinner on four days of the week. On the other three days they would start the day with a pint of cocoa (made from a quarter of an ounce of flaked cocoa or cocoa nibs sweetened with three quarters of an ounce of molasses or sugar). Dinner on those days would be soup, a pound of potatoes, six ounces of bread.

Walking through the Gaol today one realises that it was never intended to hold many prisoners. Numbers fluctuated; occasionally there were none. In April 1830, a year after the opening, there were seventeen, seven of them debtors.

The list of prisoners confined 'in the Common Gaol of the County of Anglesey this 20th day of April, 1830' makes interesting reading. This was the period when Beaumaris Gaol was well used.

Robert Owen had been in the House of Correction since 1818 for non-payment of debt. Hugh Price, too, was a debtor and as he could not maintain himself financially or by working, the County paid him fourpence a day allowance for his food. Catherine Williams earned her keep by spinning while she waited to be transported overseas, her sentence for larceny. Another who was paid fourpence a day was David Evans, convicted for larceny. Robert Hughes was imprisoned for two years for failing to produce his ship's papers to the Customs Officer at Beaumaris – he was made to shatter stones towards his maintenance. Three more debtors were in the House of Correction for short periods. William Owen, convicted of larceny, was serving three months with hard labour. John Roberts's crime of felony was considered serious enough for him to be transported. He received the County allowance while he waited to be sent overseas. Catherine Rowlands's larceny earned her two months' hard labour, although we are not told what form this took. Richard Owen shattered stones for his misdemeanours.

In 1852 the Report listed only five prisoners.

Hard labour for men took the form of oakum picking, shattering stones and later, walking the treadwheel.

Women cleaned the prison, worked in the laundry, spun, made mats, or sewed. When a woman had her baby in prison with her there was a contraption whereby she could rock the cradle in the sleeping room above by means of a cord passing through a hole in the ceiling to the cradle.

For stone-shattering, the governor had a delivery of large stones dropped in the yard where the men would work, breaking them into small pieces which were sold to be used to fill pot holes in the Anglesey roads. This was back-breaking, shoulder-aching work. Picking oakum was a tedious affair, one which wore the finger ends until they were sore. Bundles of pieces of ship's cable were made available, cut into short lengths. These had to be unravelled and the resulting strands were used for caulking for ships. Some of the pieces were knotted twine, very difficult to loosen. There were sweepings from the floor and some tarred pieces which must have been particularly difficult to handle. Today's visitors to the men's workroom can read an account of oakum picking. Both these activities had to be carried out in silence. The hours were long, with little respite to break the day.

In 1867 a treadwheel was mounted in one of the yards where it can still be seen. This was the type of hard labour most dreaded. In Beaumaris the treadwheel was connected to the prison water tank on the roof, the action of the wheel turning would pump up water from a well to replenish the tank. Prisoners 'walked' the wheel for four hours in one day, in quarter hour shifts. It was exhausting and dangerous. Once on the wheel, the worker had to keep on treading the steps otherwise he would find himself being drawn in to the workings as the wheel continued to turn without him. It was estimated that a prisoner would tread the equivalent of one and a half miles a day.

Prisoners also had to clean their cells, workrooms and corridors at least once a week and scrape down and limewash walls and ceilings every six months.

After the Prison Act of 1865 cells were heated so much of the work done previously in workrooms was carried on there. Prisoners then began to eat, work and sleep in their cells, leaving them only for a short period to exercise in the prison yard. There was no conversation. It was a gloomy, lonely existence.

Divine Service was held in the chapel on a Sunday. The stark little chapel still has its pews and pulpit and tattered Bible. The Rules for Attendance, hanging on the wall, leave no doubt as to the importance attached to religion in the life of the prison . . .

'Prisoners under charge or convicted of any crime and prisoners receiving any allowance from the county or employment from the county shall attend divine service on Sundays and at all times when such service is performed unless previously by illness or by other reasonable cause to be allowed by the Keeper, or unless their attendance shall be dispensed with by one of the visiting Justices. Debtors not attending shall be locked up for security during the time of service in such place as the Keeper may think convenient for that purpose.'

'The chaplain shall note in his Journal the absence of any prisoner from Divine Service with the cause noted. No gaming shall be permitted and the Keeper shall seize and destroy all dice, cards or any other instruments of gambling.'

Any attending worshipper, mind wandering during the chaplain's sermon, would be admonished by catching sight of the text hanging on the wall of this grim little chapel – 'Repent, for the day of judgement is at hand'.

The recommendation to improve heating and give every prisoner a cell to himself was carried out. Previously more than one would share a 'sleeping room'.

Prisoners were locked in their cells overnight, but spent the day in the workrooms – one for men, the other for women. This appertained until 1865 when the government undertook full responsibility for British prisons. From then the improvements suggested forty years earlier in the case of Beaumaris had to be carried out. Each cell was fitted with either a bed or a hammock, an enamel wash basin, a lavatory flushed by water from the roof tank. There also had to be a table and a seat. Gas lighting had been installed in 1857. An alarm was fitted to each cell so that the prisoner could attract the attention of the gaoler in an emergency. This was operated by a knob which, when pressed, rang a bell in the corridor outside the cell. This, in turn, activated a flap showing the cell number. Cells could only be opened from the outside.

One cell had no such amenity. This was the punishment cell, soundproof and secured by three separate doors. A page from the Misconduct Book for April 1849 lists the miscreants, their ages, offences and punishments . . .

'March 20: Ralph Williams, 14: cursing, swearing and other misdemeanors against prison rules; two days in solitary confinement on bread and water.
May 15: George Smith, 23; concealing a sledge hammer hidden under his bed, with intent of either murder or breaking the iron bars of his bed cell; three days in solitary cell on bread and water.'

Apparently this punishment did little to reform George Smith as in July he was committed to the same cell again, this time for 'refusing to work and being insolent to the Governor'.

Many prisoners in Beaumaris Gaol during the 1800s were uneducated. The Prison Act of 1865 ordered that inmates should be taught reading, writing and arithmetic. How much use this was to short-stay prisoners is doubtful, but maybe it sowed a seed for a wish for improvement on release.

Monthly visits to the prison were allowed to those whose sentences were for more than one month. A careful record was kept by the Keeper, noting the name of the visitor, his purpose and his relationship with the prisoner. Any package brought in to the gaol was searched in case it contained anything which might help an escape.

Prisoners under sentence of death were allowed more visitors. The record shows that these came 'to pray with the convicted man'.

Beaumaris prison was extended in 1866. A local historian, E.A. Williams, commented in her book *The Day Before Yesterday* that one of the reasons was the number of seamen held prisoner there. 'It was a common occurrence for ships to put in to Holyhead in order to land striking sailors,' she wrote. 'These would be sent to Beaumaris to await trial and their incarceration involved much expenditure for the county.'

Eventually the House of Correction was disbanded. During the following decade the administration changed as the Home Office took over responsibility for all prisons. Another Prison Act of 1877 brought yet more change as it was decided to close over thirty small prisons. Beaumaris was one. The prisoners were transferred to Caernarfon.

A few months after the closure, the county bought the Steeple Lane prison building and it began a new life as a police station. During both world wars a number of prisoners of war were housed here.

Although improvements in the prison service were

made over many years, Beaumaris Gaol was always a grim, inhospitable place. A prisoner's life was hard, but the working days of those who administered were anything but pleasant also. In winter it was cold and dark. Reading Quarter Sessions records for 1866 one can sympathise with the plight of the turnkey who applied to the Justices for more clothing. The record states grudgingly 'the clothing of the latter for the year to include a top coat – but not every year'.

Warrants and Sentences

Judging by records still existent at the Llangefni Record Office, it seems that the Beaumaris Gaol in Steeple Lane was occupied, in the main, by those awaiting trial, debtors, vagrants and beggars, those accused of bastardy, and others who were serving short term sentences for petty crime ordered by the Court at Quarter Sessions.

In the days before a national police force, it was the responsibility of the High and Petty Constables to apprehend a suspected criminal, a warrant to that effect being issued by a Justice once the charge had been made.

The catalogue of documents concerning law and order in Beaumaris lists many letters, bills for materials for the building of the new Gaol, prison inspectors' reports, advertisements for staff, but by far the most numerous are Court Orders dated between 1831 and 1849 which give an insight into the type of cases dealt with in the Court House.

In 1816 the Court Order described Richard Owen of Amlwch as an 'incorrigible rogue' and 'vagabond'. The official report of the case reads . . .

'TRINITY QUARTER 1816 . . . Whereas Richard Owen late of the Parish of Amlwch in the said County of Anglesey, labourer, a rogue (and vagabond) was duly convicted before the Reverend Hugh Wynne Jones, Clerk, one of His Majesty's Justices of the Peace, for the said County of Anglesey, for that he the said Richard Owen did run away and leave his wife and Children burthensome to the said Parish of Amlwch and was adjudged by the said Hugh Wynne Jones to be committed to the House of Correction of the said County of Anglesey until the then next Quarter Sessions of the Peace to be holden in and for the said County of Anglesey then and there to be further dealt with according to Law.

AND WHEREAS the Justices present assembled at this General Quarter Sessions of the Peace upon examination of the circumstances of the case Do adjudge the said Richard Owen to be an incorrigible rogue and vagabond.

AND IS ORDERED THAT the said Richard Owen be kept and detained in the said House of Correction or Common Gaol of the said County of Anglesey to hard labour for the space of six months from this Quarter Sessions.'

There are many warrants, similar to the following, which ordered the constables to search for and apprehend fathers of illegitimate children, charged by the Poor Law Overseers for that particular town or village who might otherwise be forced to pay to maintain the mothers and children.

'Anglesey
To Wit . . . 1829 . . . To the Petty Constables of the parish of Llandyfrydog and the Keeper of the Common Gaol in Beaumaris.

WHEREAS Jane Morris of the parish of Llandyfrydog in the said county, in her voluntary examination taken in writing, upon Oath, the twenty first day of October last before William Pritchard Lloyd Esquire, one of His Majesty's Justices of the Peace in and for the said County, hath declared herself to be with child and that the said child is likely to be born a Bastard and to be chargeable to the said Parish of Llandyfrydog, and hath charged John Owen of the Parish of Liverpool in the County of Lancaster with having gotten her with child, of the said child.'

'AND WHEREAS the said John Owen being now personally present before me, being brought by Owen Owens' (he was the Petty Constable and also assistant overseer of the Poor for Llandyfrydog) ' . . . THESE are therefore to command you, the said Constable, to take and convey the said John Owen to the Common Gaol at Beaumaris in the said County and to deliver him to the Keeper thereof, with this warrant and I do hereby command you the said Keeper of the said Gaol to receive the said John Owen into your custody in the said Gaol and him there safely to keep until he shall give such Security or enter into such Recognizance as aforesaid, or be otherwise delivered from thence.

Signed W.P. Lloyd.'

In this case the father had been found and dealt with. John Owen may have been a sailor on a brief shore leave when his ship put in to an Anglesey port. Could the child be an ancestor of someone living in Anglesey today?

In 1830 Owen Williams refused to maintain his wife and daughters, so they were forced to 'go on the Parish'. He was sent to the House of Correction for a month. Edward Jones of Llanbadrig was sent to Gaol for three months as he had refused to pay towards the lying-in costs of his partner, and the sum expected of him to the Overseer of the Poor of the parish, following her confinement. He would be released as and when he paid.

Constables on the west side of the island were to arrest David Jones, a labourer, who 'carried away a Petticoat, two aprons and one Handkerchief belonging to Mary Jones of Trefdraeth and one tablecloth belonging to John

Roberts'. He was kept in Gaol until his trial at the next Quarter Sessions.

The story of Catherine Williams began when, in 1827, she stole one purple glass cream jug of the value of 1/3d, one chamber pot of the value of five pence, one hat, 3/6d. The Keeper was commanded to keep her 'until she shall be discharged by due Course of Law'. Catherine went before the Court early in 1828 and the Court Order following her trial reads ...

'WHEREAS the above named Catherine Williams was at this present General Quarter Sessions tried and convicted of each of the above several larcenies it is ordered by this Court that the same Catherine Williams be transported beyond the seas as His Majesty shall be pleased and lawfully directed for the space of seven years.'

Debtors were arrested and taken in to the House of Correction until they could honour their debts, some of them very small.

Vagrants and beggars were given short shrift. A Court Order regarding Thomas Stone who had been sleeping rough in a lime kiln at Llannerch-y-medd despatched him to the House of Correction for fourteen days, during which time he had to undertake hard labour.

In 1829 Catherine Evans, a servant from Bryngwran, had absconded from her employment and the disappearance was reported to the Justices by her mistress. Catherine was found, appeared in Court, and was given a sentence of six weeks with hard labour.

The House of Correction saw a more unusual inmate when, in December 1829, Robert Hughes, master of the ship *Lydia* mentioned in a previous chapter, was arrested as he had failed or refused to hand his registration papers to the port's customs officer at Beaumaris. He was fined

£100 but could not pay, so the Justice ordered the Keeper at Beaumaris Gaol to accept him as a prisoner to serve ten months unless he could pay in the meantime. One hundred pounds was a large sum of money to find in 1829.

An Order which emphasises the desperate plight of the Anglesey poor is that which called for the arrest of Ellin Davies of Amlwch, to stand trial for stealing a sheaf of corn.

A Bodedern man informed the Justices of a vagabond who 'in my presence exposed his person indecently and begged alms under false pretences'. On trial the man was found guilty and ordered to be taken to the Gaol to serve for one month.

Gaynor, the wife of Robert Jones stole a quart of milk. She was sent to Beaumaris Gaol for 'one calendar month and there to be kept at hard labour'.

Children and the Court

The fate of children who broke the law was hard indeed. In 1877 a boy aged under fourteen, William Owen, appeared in court where it was decided he was a juvenile delinquent, out of control, and the court washed its hands of him, sending him for two years to the training ship *Clio*.

Although *Clio* was officially a training ship, moored in the Menai Strait, in reality she was a prison. The boys led a life of hard work, harsh treatment and drill, aimed to beat them into submission. They scrubbed decks and learned some of the basic skills of seamanship under extremely hard conditions. Anglesey mothers would warn their children that they would be sent to the *Clio* if they misbehaved.

The latter half of the 19th century was a bad time for the children at Beaumaris court. In 1850 William Jones, aged fourteen, stole a shilling at Holyhead, for which he had to work a month's hard labour followed by several years at a reform school. James Frances, aged eighteen, stole 3½d. He was sentenced to be whipped with twelve strokes of the birch after which he, too, was sent to a reform school, for three years. The same year, 1870, James Casey, aged eight, stole half a pound of sugar and some bread and butter at Llannerch-y-medd. He was whipped with six strokes of the birch and was given two weeks hard labour.

Richard Owen, aged thirteen, succumbed to temptation when he stole two bottles of sweets and two bottles of hair oil with another boy. His sentence was twelve strokes of the birch.

Three teenagers, two of eighteen and one thirteen, pleaded guilty to two indictments charging them with larceny. There were four prisoners in custody, but the fourth did not appear at the trial as he was suffering from smallpox. One of the charges, said the chairman of the Bench, was very serious as it involved breaking in to an outhouse. Their reputation had preceded their appearance in court.

They were well known as 'part of an idle, disorderly and thievish gang which Bangor had the honour of claiming as its citizens'. The boys had been employed during the summer 'in nightly depredations' and the Bench had discussed transportation as a possible sentence, but considering their ages they sentenced the two older boys to six months in prison with hard labour on each indictment, and 'the younger sentenced to two months on each, and to be twice privately whipped'.

It would be interesting to know whether their sentences had any effect upon their behaviour in later life.

The exhibition at Beaumaris castle shows this illustration of how the fort would have looked when it was the enforcer of the English crown's laws in the thirteenth century.

The ruins of Beaumaris castle today.

Beaumaris Gaol today – now a heritage centre.

A Victorian gaol warden.　　　　　*The hard-labour yard.*

The barred cell windows and yard.

The gallows door in the Gaol.

The Gaol's chapel.

Many of Beaumaris Gaol's inmates were poor people caught poaching on gentry land.

The forbidding Gaol entrance.

The central corridor in the Gaol.

An artist's impression of the scaffold.

Restraining chains

One of the cells, with toilet en suite.

Men work the treadwheel while others wait their turn.

A prisoner works at a rough loom.

A prisoner suffers a whipping.

Roll call at the prison.

Punishing stocks on display at the gaol's entrance today.

Used

AMLWCH

𝕬𝖘𝖘𝖔𝖈𝖎𝖆𝖙𝖎𝖔𝖓

FOR THE PROSECUTION OF FELONS,

1st MARCH, 1822.

WHEREAS by an Act of Parliament passed in the 1st Year of the Reign of King George the Fourth, " for the summary Punishment, in certain " cases, of Persons wilfully or maliciously damaging or committing Tres- " passes on public or private Property,"—

IT IS ENACTED, That if any Person or Persons shall wilfully or ma- liciously do or commit any Damage, Injury, or Spoil, to or upon any Building, Fence, Hedge, Gate, Stile, Tree, Wood, Underwood, Orchard, Garden, Nursery Ground, Crops, Vegetables, Plants, Land, or other Matter or Thing growing or being thereon, or to or upon real or personal property of any kind soever, and shall be thereof convicted in the manner in the said Act set forth, shall forfeit and pay to the Person or Persons aggrieved, such a Sum of Money, not exceeding £ 5, as therein directed; and in default of Payment of the same, and Expenses, the Justice convicting the Party shall and may commit the Offender or Offenders to the common Gaol, there to be kept to hard Labour for three Months, &c.   Therefore

NOTICE IS HEREBY GIVEN,

That the Members of the above Association are determined to avail themselves of the Benefit of the above Act, by prosecuting and punishing all such Offenders as they shall find guilty of committing any of the Trespasses therein set forth.

ROBT. PRICHARD,

Treasurer and Secretary to the said Association.

PRINTED AT THE OFFICE OF E. JONES, LLANERCHYMEDD.

A public notice from the Amlwch Association for the Prosecution of Felons.

Penrhyn Safnes (Gallows Point) in Beaumaris bay where pirates and smugglers'
corpses were left to rot as a warning to passing seamen.

Beaumaris Court – also open to the public.

The judge's effigy at the Court House.

The elegant magistrate's room at the Court House.

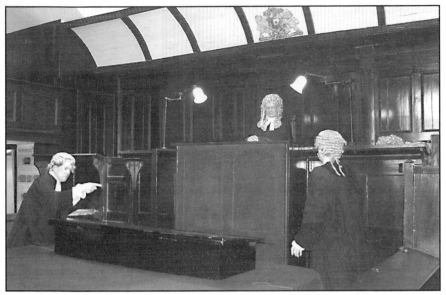

A court scene re-created inside the building today.

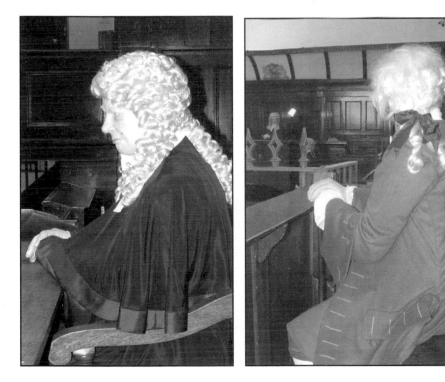

The hanging of William Murphy.

The renowned case of the wreckers of Crigyll was tried at Beaumaris Court and smugglers (below) were also frequently accused there.

The court in session – models provide realism.

The coat of arms above the judge's chair at the Court House.

At the Court's entrance today.

The old heavy door on display.

y Llong Gosbi

The Punishment Ship

H.M.S. Clio, the old punishment ship.

The Assize Court

Much pomp was attached to the twice-yearly Assizes held before a circuit Judge at Beaumaris Court House. Visitors to the Court House today see a set of Judge's robes, one of several worn depending on the type of case to be heard and the season of the year.

An Assize Judge would possess four sets, two for winter and two for summer. If he was to hear a criminal case, his robes would be scarlet. He would wear a different colour for civil cases. On the first day of Court the Judge would arrive in procession, sumptuously dressed in full-bottomed wig, breeches, silk stockings and court shoes, preceded by a trumpeter to underline the importance of the occasion. For the more businesslike sessions he would wear his everyday dress with a winged collar and bands underneath.

Defendants who did not understand English were under a disadvantage in Court, as proceedings would have to be heard in English for the Judge's benefit and then translated into Welsh so that he or she could make suitable replies to questions. Only ten of the sixty-four Judges appointed in Wales at one period understood Welsh.

The 19th century, before the closure of the Beaumaris Gaol, saw varied activity at the Assize Court. Some of the Court Orders still exist.

In 1836 William Parry, aged 56, appeared before the

Judge on two indictments, one of misdemeanour and another of assault and riot when it was claimed he obstructed the Sheriff's officers in the execution of their duty. The Court Order does not say where this happened. William Parry was sent to Beaumaris Gaol for nine months and, on release, 'bound in his own recognizance in the Sum of £200 to keep the Peace and be of good behaviour for the further period of five years'.

Parry's son was also in Court, presumably involved in the same affray, but he had surrendered himself and pleaded guilty. He was discharged 'on entering into his own Recognizance in One Hundred Pounds and two sureties of £15. He was to appear at the next Assizes to receive the judgement of the Court, 'to keep the Peace, and be of good behaviour for the term of five years'.

There is no record of the outcome, but doubtless the Court would have been lenient as he had already confessed his sins.

Transportation was still a possibility for some. Henry Jones was one who was transported for seven years after serving one month's hard labour in the House of Correction for Larceny.

Evan Morgan and Ellis Williams were transported 'for the term of their natural lives'. They had been convicted of manslaughter. Yet what mitigating circumstances caused three men, also convicted of manslaughter, not to receive similar punishment but to be imprisoned and set to hard labour, we have no record.

Forgery could result in a prison sentence, as in the case of Ellen Jones who had 'forged a Bill of Exchange for £20'. She was sentenced to serve three months' hard labour.

Not all those charged to appear in Court were convicted. In March 1847 six were discharged due to insufficient evidence being presented.

In the following year John Rowlands was charged and convicted of serious assault when he was accused of 'throwing oil of vitriol with intent to burn'. In the words of the Court Order he was ordered 'to pay a fine to the Queen of Five Pounds and to be imprisoned until paid'.

Whipping was still a form of punishment in 1832, when four men were convicted of stealing goods from a warehouse. They were sentenced to be 'severally imprisoned in the House of Correction and kept to hard labour for a space of twelve calendar months and during that time to be once severally and privately whipped'.

Some cases of larceny were tried at Quarter Sessions. It appears that if the goods stolen were above a certain value the case would go to the Assizes – as when Owen Jones was found guilty of stealing 'from a dwelling house above the value of Five Pounds'. He received sentence of 'transportation for the period of his natural life'. Margaret Williams had stolen goods of similar value. She received the same sentence.

There are several references to transportation in Beaumaris Court records. Since the colonies had been acquired during the reign of Queen Elizabeth I there was a need for men and women to maintain and develop the local industries there, and the convict population answered that need. Sending convicts abroad lessened the demand for prison cells. It was a case of 'out of sight, out of mind'. But as the colonies began to be self-supporting, workers from Britain were no longer needed. In 1853 the colonies refused to accept more, and the practice was abolished by law that year. Until the American War of Independence America had accepted convicts to the penal settlements. In 1788 the first batch sailed for Botany Bay in New South Wales. Felons continued to be sent there until 1840, when Tasmania became the only colony still willing to accept them.

Local newspapers during the reign of Queen Victoria carried detailed reports of cases heard at Quarter Sessions and Assizes, under the heading 'Local and Provincial

Intelligence'. Reading them today, they are colourful reminders of the sad stories which resulted in incarceration in Beaumaris Gaol.

'ROBBERY FROM A STEAM BOAT . . . William Williams, a young man, pleaded guilty to having, on the night of the 7th of December, entered the steamship Mersey, then moored at Llandisilio, or Menai Bridge, and stolen a jacket, with some money, the property of the steward of the vessel, and afterwards secreted himself in the captain's berth, where he was found with the stolen property in his possession. The court sentenced the prisoner to six months imprisonment with hard labour.'

. . . in another issue, the Chairman of the Bench is reported as drawing a picture of crime then being perpetrated . . .

'The Chairman, in opening his address to the Grand Jury, observed that the number of bills before them for theft of different description, was large, and this would give them something like an insight into the state of the county at the present time. He could not say that Crime of great magnitude had been committed, but petty crime had been carried out to an extent never been known before in the county; but it was gratifying to find that these offences were not committed by the inhabitants but by that class of persons termed "tramps".'

The Ultimate Sentence

From existing records there appear to have been several executions in Beaumaris before the Gaol in Steeple Lane closed, but only two at the Gaol itself. Before 1829 hangings took place either within the castle walls or to the west of the town in the area known as Gallows Point, today more famous for sailing.

It will be seen from the list of those executed in Beaumaris since the 15th century that the death penalty could be the sentence for a variety of crimes, some of them comparatively inoffensive to us today. At one period death by hanging was a sentence which could be passed quite indiscriminately, for no fewer than two hundred different charges. This appertained for many years until, in the 19th century, the situation was beginning to concern the public.

During the 18th and 19th centuries punishments were unrealistically harsh and Anglesey juries would find the slightest reason for lessening the verdict wherever possible.

In a letter to the *Morning Herald* in 1830 a correspondent claimed that 'laws attended with too severe penalties defeat their own object'. He quoted a case heard in the Caernarfon court of a man charged with forgery yet acquitted, when one of the jurymen later admitted 'Neither my fellow jurymen nor myself had the least doubt of the prisoner's guilt but we were unwilling to bring in a verdict of guilty because we were aware the prisoner would have been punished with death, a penalty which we conceived to be too severe for the offence'. The same opinion was held countrywide.

Bribing the jury was not unknown, and was thought to be the reason for the acquittal of Evan Evans when he was tried for murder in Beaumaris in 1824.

Near Brynsiencyn an illegitimate child was snatched from his cradle while the mother was out milking. The father of the child, Evan Evans, worked at a neighbouring farm. A woman living close by swore she saw Evans returning with a parcel under his arm. Witnesses saw him crossing the Strait with the ferry from Barras that same morning but nothing further was heard of him for several weeks. He was eventually arrested in Flint and brought back to Beaumaris for trial. The child's body had been found lying under straw at Llyslew, the farm where he had been working on the day the child was missed. The evidence seemed watertight, but the jury acquitted him and people in the area around Brynsiencyn believed that his family had bribed the jurors.

The list of those hanged at Beaumaris is long and the charges are varied.

In 1468 seven brothers were hanged after being found guilty of murder and robbery.

In 1593, following two trials, a Catholic priest, William Davies, met his end at Beaumaris at a time of widespread Catholic persecution. His trial was held when he was charged with planning to send recruits to the priesthood to Valladolid via Ireland. He and his associates were intercepted and arrested. One of the party, a prominent Catholic named Robert Pugh, escaped while they were in captivity in Holyhead, but Davies and four would-be students were removed to Beaumaris for safer custody. Davies was imprisoned in a dungeon at the castle, to await the arrival of a Judge from London.

At his trial he was found guilty of treason, but local people created such a stir at the verdict that the Judge was forced to postpone sentence, and the prisoner was removed to Shropshire, then the centre of Welsh administrative affairs, before being returned to Beaumaris for a re-trial and eventual sentence. Such was the high feeling in Beaumaris that an executioner could not be found locally, nor wood for the gallows nor any of the necessary items for carrying out the execution. Two men were hired from Chester, but nobody in the town was prepared to give them lodging. Materials had to be brought in from outside. Eventually all was in place, and William Davies was hanged, drawn and quartered on July 27, 1593.

Being accused and found guilty of witchcraft led to the death of Margaret uch Richard in 1655, when she was said to have cast a spell on a neighbour who later died.

There were four executions at Beaumaris in the 18th century, the first taking place in 1719 when 17-years-old Thomas Esay of Beddgelert had several charges to answer, including stealing a horse. He was found guilty and the death sentence was carried out. A year later, Sian uch Evan of Llanddaniel was hanged for robbery. Joseph and Robin, two tinkers, lost their lives after charges against them of robbing Llantysilio church were proved, as did an unnamed Irishwoman hanged for attempted murder at Bodedern.

Sheep stealing at Llanallgo led John Jones to the scaffold in 1786. Three years later John Ellise was found guilty of house breaking at Pontrhydpont. He suffered a similar fate.

When the Steeple Lane gaol opened it was intended that executions should take place there, and a condemned cell was prepared on the first floor. This was twice the size of the other prison cells. It contained a fireplace and was furnished with the bare necessities. The passage outside led to a door in the outer wall which, when appropriate, opened on to the scaffold which was a specially erected platform above the street.

The first man condemned to be hanged at the new gaol, in 1830, was William Griffith for, as a local newspaper described, 'a most brutal and inhuman attempt to murder his wife'. How the newspaper relished the story, and, no doubt, coloured it to some extent.

William Griffith was separated from his wife, but one evening visited the house in Newborough where she was living with her daughter. The frightened girl ran to a neighbour for help, and when they returned Griffith had left. Her mother was found with her head beneath the grate, covered with hot coals. She was still alive, but severely burned.

After his trial Griffith was incarcerated in the new prison where he was allowed to receive visitors. The newspaper reported efforts made to persuade him to admit to his crime and seek God's forgiveness . . .

'Although all possible means for his conversion were unceasingly used by the Rev. H.D. Owen, the chaplain of the Gaol, the Rev. Mr Hughes, Beaumaris, and several other individuals who took a pious interest in his spiritual welfare, we are truly sorry to say that to all human appearance he died as he had lived, without any manifestation of Christian feeling or even of manly firmness.'

While in prison, Griffith was mentally disturbed and violent. The long newspaper report continued . . .

'On the morning of the execution, having been for a few minutes left alone, he tore up the wooden bench on which his bed was placed, and fixing it against the door for some time prevented all access from without.

The door being at length forced, he was secured and every effort which humanity and Christian feeling could suggest having been in vain used to compose his mind, the requisite preparations were made for carrying the sentence of the law into execution, the criminal all the while uttering the most agonising cries and groans.'

Griffith put up a struggle to the end, attacking the executioner until he was pinioned and led to the gallows.

'The melancholy fate of this unhappy man presents a frightful picture of the close of an irreligious and immoral life by a violent and ignominious death, and we sincerely hope will operate as an awful warning to those who are weak enough to deceive themselves into the damning belief that it is an easy thing at the last hour to obtain that grace which they despise in the course of their life.'

Executions in the 19th century were public events until the Prison Act of 1865 declared they should be private, carried out within the precincts of a gaol. After the closure of Beaumaris Gaol in 1877 executions took place in Caernarfon.

In the case of William Griffith, 'an immense multitude' was said to have gathered. Those in business – shopkeepers, hoteliers and inn keepers – were kept busy all day. But there was still some doubt in the minds of local people that the death penalty should have been passed on William Griffith, as his wife was still alive. The Sheriff, it was said, feared an uprising and brought in more constables to control the crowd. Men refused to work on building the scaffold so once again labour had to be brought in, this time from Liverpool. The executioner came from Chester.

The cost of an execution was borne by H.M. Treasury, following an obsequious appeal from the local sheriff for remuneration. This had to be made in detail so that government officers could be sure they were not being overcharged. Following the execution of William Griffith the Sheriff charged £6.6.0 to Chester and back to obtain the services of an executioner. He paid him a retainer of £3. Further £7 was paid for the Deputy Sheriff's hiring of a coach to fetch the executioner to Beaumaris and for 'expenses on the road'. Because local people refused to erect the gallows and make the coffin, £1013.00 was spent to fetch men from Liverpool, and to pay them. Eight yards of black cloth to cover the gallows cost £2.16.0. The executioner received £17 for hanging the prisoner. Seven guineas was spent on procuring special constables and 'Javelin men' to ensure security and the good behaviour of the crowd. The grave digger received £1.1.0. Ancillary expenses totalled five guineas, making a grand total of £61.12.0.

The legal report of the charge and the trial makes heavy reading, but it is reproduced here as it provides the atmosphere of the proceedings as they took place in 1830 . . .

'Whereas the said William Griffith was at this present Great Sessions and General Gaol Delivery indicted arraigned and tried for that he did on the Second day of April last past with force and arms at the parish of Llanbeder Newborough in the said County in and upon the said Mary Griffith feloniously unlawfully and maliciously make an assault and then and there with both the Hands of him the said William Griffith put about the Neck and throat of the said Mary Griffith then and there feloniously unlawfully and maliciously did fix and fasten and with both his Hands so fixed and fastened about the Neck and throat of her the said

Mary Griffith then and there feloniously unlawfully and maliciously did attempt to strangle and suffocate with intent thereby then and there in so doing and by means thereof feloniously unlawfully and of his malice aforethought to murder her the said Mary Griffith and then and there with a certain stick which he had and held in his Hand then and there feloniously, unlawfully and maliciously did force into the Mouth of her the said Mary Griffith and did thereby feloniously and unlawfully endeavour to force the said Stick down the throat of her the said Mary Griffith and in so doing by forcing the said Stick down the throat of her the said Mary Griffith then and there feloniously unlawfully and maliciously wound the said Mary Griffith and to do her some grievous bodily harm against the form of the Statute in that case made and provided and upon his Trial found Guilty thereof.'

'It is therefore ordered by this Court that the said William Griffith for the said crime be from thence taken back to the Common Gaol of the said County the place from whence he came, and from thence on the fifteenth day of September now next ensuing to the Common place of Execution in this County and there be hanged by the Neck until he be dead.

Signed by High Sheriff of the County of Anglesey.'

Two years later Hugh Owen suffered the death penalty for stealing sheep and in 1833 Robert Brown met his end similarly, for house breaking. Intent to do grievous bodily harm could result in the death penalty, as it did for David Williams in 1835 after he was found guilty of maliciously stabbing.

The *Caernarfon & Denbigh Herald* of 1862 carried a long report on the final hours of Richard Rowlands of Llanfaethlu who had been found guilty of murdering his father-in-law, an act he denied until the end. Had he been tried today the outcome could well have been different, as it is now believed that the evidence was insufficient to convict him.

Dic Rowlands, as he was known, had married a widow who had children. After the marriage he did not live with his wife, but continued working as a farm labourer, moving from farm to farm wherever he could find employment. His wife continued to live in her old home where she cared for her elderly father.

Rowlands had a reputation for being immoral, showing scant acknowledgement of the law. He believed that his father-in-law was intending to banish the family from his home, and Dic determined to take his revenge on the old man as he followed him one night when he went to visit a neighbour. Richard Williams's body was later found in a ditch.

At the trial in Beaumaris Court House he denied murder but the jury thought otherwise, although Anglesey juries were sometimes very reluctant to convict for capital crimes as they hated sending their compatriots to their death.

The newspaper reported in detail the last days of the convicted man, information divulged to the reporter through the diary of the Rev. Hugh Hughes, Calvinistic minister at Beaumaris who visited Richard Rowlands daily, along with other local clergymen, to pray with him and exhort him to seek God's forgiveness for his past life.

'After the sentence', wrote the reporter, 'the prisoner did not appear to have suffered any loss of appetite until the evening preceding his execution, when he declined to partake of supper. He also refused to take breakfast on the fatal day. On Thursday night he slept soundly until about twelve o'clock. At four he was visited by Mr Davies and J. Williams Esq., the Under

Sheriff, who were unremitting in their attention to him. At about half past five they were joined by Mr Hughes. The reverend gentlemen remained with him to the last, encouraging him to trust in the atonement of his Saviour and praying fervently on his behalf. The poor man was deeply affected and professed to have acted upon the instruction of his counsellors, but still asserted in the most impressive way his innocence of the murder. One of his last acts was to take the hands of his two faithful friends in his own, and then solemnly exclaim – 'Remember my last words; I tell you I am innocent of the crime for which I have been condemned.'

The executioner was William Calcroft who was nearing the end of a long career as public hangman.

'He is a man of middle height,' the reporter wrote of Calcroft, 'rather broad-set, his countenance is not at all repulsive but has that fixedness of outline which is common to persons who perform deeds requiring great nerve. His Hair is rather grey and he wears his whiskers, which are considerably whiter than the hair of his head, and rather long, all round his face. He would pass for a respectable Englishman of ordinary moral stamp.'

The execution of Richard Rowlands drew the crowds who arrived in every conceivable form of transport, from the nearby villages and from across the Strait. The boys of the Grammar School were given a day's holiday and taken elsewhere so that they would not see the event.

'The road from the Garth Ferry was a mighty stream of humanity – or more properly speaking, perhaps, of inhumanity. As early as four o'clock they began to assemble in the vicinity of the gaol, and before the hour appointed for the execution an immense number had congregated in the churchyard, on the church walls, and in every available place in the locality . . . we are happy to state that although a great number of persons were assembled, the greatest decorum prevailed which was no doubt owing in a great measure to the excellent police arrangements.'

A legend has grown around this last tragic hanging. It is said the face of the church clock opposite the Gaol has never since told the correct time.

The arbitrary use of the death penalty was evident in several cases where murderers were not hanged. In 1863 a Pencarnisiog man was fatally shot by a friend, a militiaman. The soldier was declared insane and sent to an asylum. Two brothers fought in a drunken orgy near Malltraeth, one knifing the other. The murderer was found guilty, not condemned to death but was instead sent to prison for a period of hard labour.

A murder trial held at Beaumaris Court House was that of William Murphy. This was in 1909, long after the Gaol closed.

Murphy, a labourer, was charged with and found guilty of the murder of his former mistress, Gwen Ellen Jones. She had left him for another man, a situation Murphy could not accept. He had threatened to kill her before actually doing so on Christmas night in 1909 but on previous occasions her child had been with her and he did not want the child to be a witness. He persuaded Gwen Ellen to meet him at the Bardsey Inn, Holyhead, and strangled her on her way home. Next day he visited her home and confessed to the murder, even taking her new lover to see the body.

Murphy pleaded insanity at the trial, but the jury was convinced that execution was the only possible end to this sordid story, and William Murphy was hanged at Caernarfon Gaol in February 1910 after a recommendation for mercy was rejected.

A trial at Beaumaris Court House during the Second World War which created a stir locally was that of Albert Arthur Nettleton. The Court House was crowded to hear the legal battle concerning the 32-years-old soldier from Ashton-under-Lyne who had killed his wife, Ivy, and buried her body in the sand at Traeth Coch *(Red Wharf Bay)* where the couple were staying on holiday.

Ivy Nettleton was found by a woman riding her horse after the tide had receded. She had been a sick woman for some time. Her sickness, it was claimed, had affected her mentally and the marriage was at breaking point. Obviously the jury was in sympathy with the young man, who had confessed to the murder. Instead of pronouncing the death sentence the Judge, in his comments, agreed with their decision and sentenced Nettleton to five years' penal servitude.

Today . . . and Tomorrow

Like many centres throughout the country which have been a warp over which the weft of history has been woven, Beaumaris Court House and Gaol have become museums. But although those passing through today do so merely out of curiosity and a wish to learn about their original purpose and not carrying the stigma of law-breaking, they still feel the palpable atmosphere permeating the buildings.

In one year some twenty thousand people have visited the two sites in tandem, first one then the other.

Ynys Môn County Council's Leisure & Heritage Department now has the responsibility for running both museums, a challenge they took from Gwynedd County Council in 1996 when the island became an autonomous administration. Since then some helpful changes have taken place in order to make interpretation even clearer, and more are envisaged.

The audio programme in the Court House is a popular feature, as it reproduces in sound one of the hearings which took place many years ago. Listening, while looking at the figure of the Judge seated at the head of the Court, one's imagination is fired and it is easy to picture the scene.

Features especially appreciated are the dramatic presentations staged by students of the Drama Department of the University at Bangor, at the Court

House and in the Gaol. They are performed daily during school and college holidays. The presentations are based on some aspect of law and order in Beaumaris. These will continue and it is hoped to enact in the square outside the Court House next season and possibly elsewhere in the town to make the museums better known to visitors.

Law and order holds a fascination for children. School groups make an important contribution to attendance figures at both buildings. A study room at the gaol is the latest addition, where displays and seating will help teachers to co-ordinate what the children see on their visits.

Those responsible for these two historic buildings, open to the public between Easter and the end of September each year, are fully aware of their importance to the social history of Beaumaris, and Anglesey.

Further reading

Beaumaris Gaol: a pack of copied documents for schools; Mary Aris and Gwynedd Archives Service.

E.A. Williams; *The Day Before Yesterday*; privately published.

A.D. Carr; *Medieval Anglesey*; pub. Anglesey Antiquarian Society.

Transactions of the Anglesey Antiquarian Society 1925: *Anglesey Sessions Records* (Hugh Owen).

Beaumaris Gaol, the county prison, 1829-1875: Ms. Sally Griffiths Ms. at Llangefni Library.

Angharad Llwyd, *A History of the Island of Mona*.

Nesta Evans, *Social Life in mid 18th century Anglesey*.

Iolo Wyn, *A history of Beaumaris*.

RCAM Anglesey.

D.N.B. (John Howard).

Acknowledgements

My thanks go to many people who have an interest in crime and punishment in Anglesey, all more knowledgeable than myself. They have been so generous in sharing their knowledge, and patient with my questioning. Also –

Ann Venables, archivist, Llangefni Record Office, and her ever-helpful staff.
Gwynedd Record Office staff at Caernarfon, for permission to quote from their publications.
John Rowlands of Four Mile Bridge for guidance on the magisterial service of days gone by.
Jean McQueen and Menai Bridge Catholic Church for information about William Davies.
Alun Gruffydd, curator at Oriel Ynys Môn who now oversees the museums at the Court House and the Gaol – for information and permission to use illustrations.
Staff at the Court House and Gaol who cheerfully answered a barrage of questions.
Myrddin ap Dafydd for illustrations.
Gwasg Carreg Gwalch for the invitation to write such an interesting story.